$16.00
3.10

Ripley's Believe It or Not!

Developed and produced by Ripley Publishing Ltd

This edition published and distributed by:
Mason Crest Publishers Inc.
370 Reed Road, Broomall, Pennsylvania 19008
(866) MCP-BOOK (toll free)
www.masoncrest.com

Ripley's Believe It or Not!
Beyond Belief
ISBN 978-1-4222-1537-1
Library of Congress Cataloging-in-Publication data is available

Ripley's Believe It or Not!—Complete 16 Title Series
ISBN 978-1-4222-1529-6

PUBLISHER'S NOTE
While every effort has been made to verify the accuracy of the entries in this book,
the Publishers cannot be held responsible for any errors contained in the work.
They would be glad to receive any information from readers.

WARNING
Some of the stunts and activities in this book are undertaken by experts and should not
be attempted by anyone without adequate training and supervision.

Printed in the United States of America

BEYOND BELIEF

PUBLISHING

a Jim Pattison Company

Beyond Belief

is a collection of staggering stories that defy the imagination. Read about the man who walked a tightrope for 22 days, the girl who married a dog, and the farmer injured by an exploding pig—all in this astonishing book.

A dog and its owner masquerade as tigers on a Florida beach...

Miraculous Survival

Ivory Hill survived an automobile accident in which a 27 in (70 cm) wooden post pierced through his chest, narrowly missing his heart!

On November 17, 1941, the 28-year-old plantation worker from New Orleans lost control of his automobile while driving at night, crashing into a bridge near Thibodeux. After the accident, Hill walked for about half a mile and then traveled by car for another 15 mi (25 km) to get help—without losing consciousness or even falling down.

Ripley's
IVORY HILL
EXHIBIT NO: 23027
WOODEN POST PIERCED HILL'S CHEST,
TAKING FIVE MEMBERS OF HOSPITAL
STAFF TO PULL OUT THE STAKE

The wooden stake narrowly missed Hill's heart and smashed one lung. Within two months he had fully recovered.

TOP FIVE
CAUSES OF ACCIDENTAL DEATH IN THE U.S.A.

1 Motor vehicle crashes
2 Falls
3 Poison (excluding food poisoning)
4 Drowning
5 Fires and burns

Paul Kosky survived having a 26-ft (8-m) long steel bar driven through his head, in an industrial accident. The bar entered through his left mandible in the jaw and exited through the top of his skull. He didn't lose consciousness and made a complete recovery, going back to work at the steel-plant soon after!

Human Missile Irving Michaels of Pennsylvania, was blown 200 ft (61 m) above his own home after crawling down a drainage pipe to ignite 5 gal (19 l) of gasoline he had poured down the pipe to smoke out a raccoon. Incredibly, he suffered only minor injuries.

Inner Bomb On April 7, 1984, professional golfer Tony Cosgrave was playing a round at Baltray near Dublin when he was struck by lightning. At the hospital, surgeons discovered that his bowel had been perforated by an explosion of gases ignited by the lightning, which probably entered his abdomen through a brass belt buckle. Cosgrave recovered to resume his golf career.

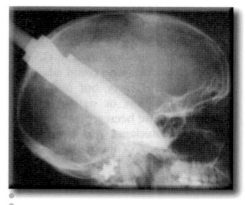

In 1997, Alison Kennedy survived being stabbed in the head in a motiveless assault while traveling by train from London to Guildford, England. The 6 in (15 cm) blade missed Kennedy's brain stem and all her major blood vessels. It took surgeons 2.5 hours to remove the knife from her skull. She was left with some numbness in one arm and a level of tunnel vision, but miraculously survived the attack.

"Fall Guy" Nicholas Fagnani survived many accidents in his lifetime. He fell 55 ft (17 m) at the age of five, 60 ft (18 m) at the age of 12, fell 20 stories from the Liberty Bank building in New York, and was later hit by a fast train that threw him 300 ft (90 m) through the air.

Mass Execution On June 22, 1918, 504 sheep were killed by a single lightning strike in the Wasatch National Forest, Utah.

What'll It Be?

In 2002, a Chinese man named Li was bitten by a preserved snake when he opened a bottle of spirits. The stopper to the bottle, which was made of cork, allowed some air in, which allowed the snake to breathe during its year-long confinement.

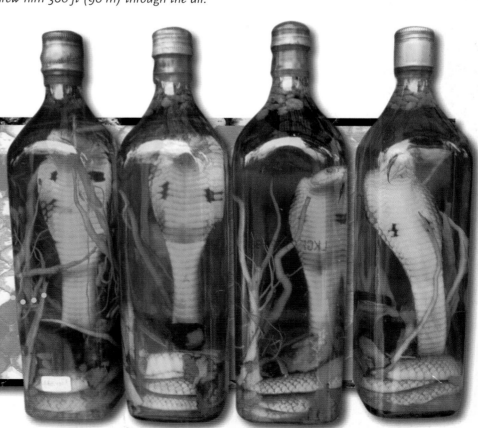

Alcoholic drinks such as rice wine containing preserved snakes or other creatures are popular in China.

An eruption of lethal carbon dioxide gas from the bottom of Cameroon's Lake Nyos in 1986 rolled 13 mi (21 km) down a valley, killing more than 1,700 people and thousands of cattle.

Unsafe at Home Gerard Hommel was a mountaineer who survived six Everest expeditions. One day, he fell off a ladder while changing a lightbulb at home in Nantes, France. He cracked his head on the sink and died.

Safely Skewered A road construction worker in Austria was skewered on an iron rod from his groin to his armpit. He phoned his wife from the ambulance to tell her not to worry—he was going to be fine. The 7-ft (2-m) rod had missed all major blood vessels and organs. Doctors told the man he would make a full recovery.

Jack Thompson was skewered by a metal pole during a car accident—and survived.

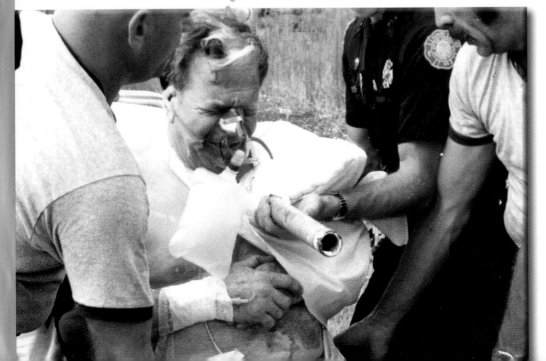

Clean Escape Window washer Kerry Burton, 27, fell five stories in Calgary, Alberta, when his rope mechanism failed. He fell onto a bucket of water, and then bounced about 2 ft (60 cm) with the bucket wedged onto his bottom. The bucket probably saved his life.

Lucky Brake In 2002, Lisa Landau, a champion horsewoman, survived 34 hours buried in a bog after her car plunged off a road in County Wicklow, Ireland. Trapped in the upturned car, Lisa survived by breathing through an air pocket she managed to find near the brake pedal.

Staying Alive Two children survived by holding on to their dead mother's body after their plane crashed into choppy seas in the Bahamas in 2003. In the same accident, a woman held her baby above her head for an hour until the U.S. Coastguard arrived.

Doesn't Add Up Travis Bogumill was shot with an industrial nail gun that drove a 3-in (8-cm) nail all the way into his skull, but he recovered and the only difference it made is that he's not quite the math whiz he used to be.

Vesna Vulovic, a stewardess on a Yugoslav DC-9 jet airliner that blew up in January 1972, survived a fall from more than 33,000 ft (10,058 m). She was paralyzed from the waist down, but later recovered and can now walk.

Shock A 25-year-old poacher in the Russian town of Tula died after putting a live electrical cable into a pond to catch fish. He forgot to disconnect the electricity before wading in to collect the fish.

Two-year-old Dwanna Lee had a miraculous escape when she was struck by a freight train and thrown 10 ft (3 m) through the air. The engine and six cars passed over her body—without injuring her.

Lover's Lock Doctors in Copenhagen spent two hours trying to pry two lovers apart after the braces on their teeth locked as they kissed passionately in a city cinema. A medic said, "It wouldn't have taken so long had they been able to stop laughing."

Stowaway Snake In 1991, a pilot lost control of his helicopter near Rock Hill, South Carolina, when he tried to step on a copperhead snake that slid out of a vent near his feet. The helicopter crashed into trees and was destroyed, and the pilot was injured.

The contents were still fresh and the ice cubes had not melted in this electric refrigerator, which was the only thing left standing after the house it was in was completely destroyed by fire.

SAFETY CUSHION

A beer belly was the hero of this man's story! Doctors who treated 264 lb (120 kg) Shaun Reaney of Birmingham, England, for serious stomach injuries inflicted by a power saw believe that his life was saved by his beer belly, which kept the blade of the saw away from his internal organs.

Death's Joy In January 2003, police in Spain chased a motorcyclist for 43 mi (69 km) at speeds of up to 112 mph (180 km/h) before he crashed. Investigators discovered that the rider had died about 30 minutes before the crash. Believe it or not, he had frozen to death.

Think Cue

Ron Fenwick was nearly snookered when he tripped onto a pile of cue sticks and was speared through the head by one of them.

When rushed to hospital, surgeons removed the cue stick by pulling it slowly out, as its shape was unlikely to cause further damage. The cue stick was not going through any organs and the only ongoing ill effects Fenwick has suffered are mild headaches and a pain in his tongue, which slightly affects his speech.

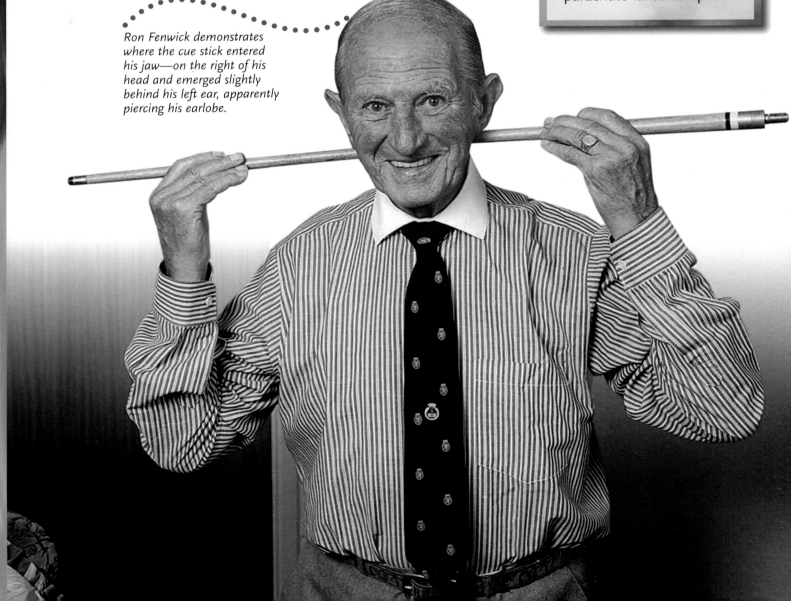

Ron Fenwick demonstrates where the cue stick entered his jaw—on the right of his head and emerged slightly behind his left ear, apparently piercing his earlobe.

SURVIVORS OF LONG FALLS

Vesna Vulovic—fell from an exploded DC-9 jetliner at 33,000 ft (10,000 m)

Mike Hussey and Amy Adams—descended 13,450 ft (4,100 m) with a torn parachute that had snagged on their aircraft's tail

Juliane Keopcke—fell over 10,000 ft (3,000 m) from her airplane in Peru

Jill Shields—freefell 9,515 ft (2,900 m) after her parachute failed to open

SNAKE SKIN COLLAR!

Biswajit Sawain woke up at his home in Bhubaneshwar, India, to find a cobra wrapped around his throat. Friends were too frightened to remove it, so after several hours Biswajit took a rickshaw to a nearby temple and prayed to the Hindu god Shiva, asking to be released from the reptile. Soon afterward, the snake relaxed its grip and slithered off.

Saved by Junk Food Trapped for a week in his wrecked car in December 2002, Robert Ward of West Virginia survived freezing temperatures by burning the car's manual page by page, and eating all the unopened tomato sauce, chilli and mayo packets he'd previously discarded on the car's floor.

Accident Prone American men are five times more likely to die by accident than women.

Coin-up Killers Vending machines caused 37 fatal accidents in the U.S.A. between 1978 and 1995.

ONE FOR THE RABBITS

Farmer Vincent Caroggio was hunting rabbits near Chartres, France. After killing five, he stopped for a rest, putting down the shotgun by his side. A rabbit bolted from its hole and stepped on the trigger, causing the gun to go off—killing the farmer.

Driven by Fate In 1975, Neville Ebin of Bermuda was killed when the moped he was riding was hit by a taxi. One year later, while riding the same moped, the man's brother was struck by the same taxi, driven by the same driver—who was carrying the very same passenger.

Kite Violence In 2003, the Mayor of Lahore in Pakistan banned kite-flying "dog fights" following a series of accidents that left 12 people dead and others injured. Some of the victims had had their throats cut by the glass-coated lines used by competitors to sever the strings of their rivals' kites.

Road Toll More people in the United States have died in car accidents than all the American soldiers who have died in wars since 1776 combined.

Steep Step While laying a telecommunications cable on the roof of a five-story office building in Walnut Creek, California, Ken Larsen walked backward over the edge, falling 65 ft (20 m) through tree branches. He suffered minor scratches and bruises.

What Train?

A woman walking on the rail tracks at Sjomarken near Boras, Sweden, was hit by an express train moving at 60 mph (96 km/h). When the train stopped and the driver and guard went out to look for a body, they found the woman staggering about on the embankment some 650 ft (200 m) away. Two days later it was discovered that the woman was a 59-year-old patient at a local hospital. She couldn't remember the accident, and had only minor bruises on her left arm and forehead.

Mrs. Hewlett Hodges of Sylacauga, Alabama, was actually hit by a meteorite on November 30, 1954. The 9 lb (4 kg) meteorite crashed through her roof, bounced off a radio, and struck her on the hip, causing severe bruising.

Cornish Miracle On July 6, 1979, an RAF Hawker Hunter jet fighter crashed into the English village of Tintagel, Cornwall. Although the village was crowded with tourists and parts of the plane landed within yards of a fuel tanker, no one was killed or seriously injured. Even the pilot, who had ejected into the sea, was picked up unharmed.

Nick of Time In 1988, U.S. parachutist Eddie Turner saved his unconscious colleague while they were both freefalling, by pulling the ripcord of his friend's parachute ten seconds before he hit the ground.

Hotrodder In 1991, Kelvin Page, a steelworker in Kent, England, was impaled through the head by a hot steel rod. He pulled it out with his bare hands after a workmate sawed it down to a manageable size.

Buried in Candy A 23-year-old candy factory worker in Marseilles, France, was crushed to death when a bin filled with 5,000 lb (2,270 kg) of marshmallows fell on him.

Fright Wig A 53-year-old man from Abbeville, France, stopped his car to try on an expensive new wig. He applied special glue and put on the wig, then lit a cigarette. The glue fumes ignited and the car exploded, killing him instantly.

Taking the Fall Both of Gareth Griffith's parachutes malfunctioned in a tandem jump with his instructor, Michael Costello, near Umatilla, Florida, in June 1997. Falling together from 5,500 ft (1,680 m), Costello maneuvered so that he would land first, cushioning Griffith's impact. Griffith survived, but Costello did not.

Office Pitfalls Official U.K. accident figures for 1999 reveal that calculators caused 37 office injuries, rubber bands hurt 402 people, and staplers injured 1,317 workers.

This sedan was cut in half in a collision, but its windows weren't even cracked!

Snake Charmer Turkish actor Sonmez Yikilmaz was sleeping in a tent when a black snake slipped into his open mouth. X-rays showed that the snake was still alive but Sonmez refused an operation to remove it. He opted for an ancient cure—hanging upside down from a tree while a pot of steaming milk was placed below him. The smell of the milk lured the creature back out through his mouth!

Early Morning Riser Asuncion Gutirrez, aged 100, startled her mourning family in Managua, Nicaragua, when she sat up in her coffin at her wake and asked for food. The family would have been even more shocked if it hadn't been the third time she had woken from the dead!

Flawed Diagnosis Englishman Kenneth Andrews was accidentally poisoned with the wrong medicine in 1930 following an appendix operation in Hong Kong, and was told he only had a short time to live. In World War II he was shot twice, stabbed, bitten by a rabid dog, and contracted malaria. He died in 1999 aged 106.

Won't Try That Again A man from Clermont, France, blew up his house when he added gasoline to a washing machine to try to remove a grease stain from his shirt. A spark ignited the gasoline, and blew out the first floor of his home, knocking him unconscious.

PIG IGNORANT
In Transylvania, pork rind is a traditional Christmas delicacy. Farmers inflate butchered pigs using a pump to stretch the skin, and then burn off the bristles. In 1990, a farmer from Cluj in Transylvania had the not-very-bright idea of pumping up his pig with butane gas. As soon as he applied a flame, the pig exploded, throwing him to the ground. He spent three days in the hospital recovering.

Twin Tragedy A tragic double accident killed twin brothers in Finland in 2002. The first brother died when hit by a truck as he was crossing the road on a bike. Two hours later and 1 mi (1.5 km) away, the second brother was killed by another truck as he crossed the same road.

HE'S NO PIKER
Dan Droessler of Platteville, Wisconsin, needed 60 stitches after a 36-in (14-cm) pike bit his foot as he dangled it over the side of his canoe on Twin Valley Lake. Droessler pulled his foot into the canoe with the pike still attached. He had to pay the Wisconsin Department of Natural Resources a $10.55 special permit fee in order to keep the fish and have it stuffed.

" Shot twice, bitten by a rabid dog, poisoned, and had malaria! "

Braving a Brushfire

Rajendra Kumar Tiwari of India demonstrates his ability to balance more than a dozen lighted candles in his moustache.

The Allahabad-based performer twirls his moustache to the rhythmic beat of traditional Indian music without twitching a muscle in the rest of his body. Tiwari says: "I stop eating or drinking anything at least two hours before a moustache dance because food makes it difficult to control your breathing, and that hurts in getting the right balance for the moustache."

Performance artist Rajendra Kumar Tiwari has even had two teeth extracted to make balancing the candles easier.

HE'S A CORKER!
John Pollack, a speechwriter for former president Clinton, sailed a boat made from 165,000 corks 165 mi (266 km) down Portugal's River Douro in 2002. Pollack has been collecting corks for 30 years but was helped on the 17-day voyage by a donation of 150,000 corks from the Cork Supply Company of California.

Someone's Barking In 2003, Indianapolis dog lover Ilia Macdonald purchased a luxury bathroom for her french poodle, Pierre Deux. His toilet lid is wrapped in chiffon with a purple feather boa border and the room is adorned with a specially commissioned $400 painting that features a note supposedly written by Pierre to his girlfriend Gigi. Pierre relieves himself on disposable diapers arranged on the floor.

OBSESSIVE BEHAVIOR

- Rather than spotting trains, a man from Yorkshire, England, spots cement mixers

- A paranoid man from Oxnard, California, was so convinced that police were watching him that he dissected his pet guinea pig to remove what he believed was a hidden camera!

- A man from Leicestershire, England, transformed his flat into the interior of the *Starship Enterprise*

Up a Tree A couple who lived in a tree house near San Francisco for 12 years were finally evicted in 2002. Besh Serdahely, 58, and Thelma Cabellero, 50, met at a San Francisco soup kitchen and originally spent their honeymoon in the tree before making it their home.

Daredevil Dachshund Skydiver Ron Sirull performed at the Air and Space Show at Vandenberg Air Force Base, California, in 2002—accompanied by his pet dachshund. "Brutus the Skydiving Dog," as he is billed, wears goggles and rides in Sirull's jumpsuit and, according to his owner, is "totally turned on" by the experience.

Pickle Pride Residents of a village in Michigan hold an annual parade to celebrate Christmas pickles. The specialities of the festival, staged in Berrien Springs, are chocolate-covered gherkins.

Laying Down the Law Judge John Prevas of the Baltimore Circuit was so angry when vital evidence at an attempted murder trial in August 2002 wasn't handed in on time that he ordered Detective Michael Baier to do 25 push-ups in court!

In 1934, four-year-old Billy Crawford made several gigantic leaps in Cleveland, Ohio, while he was harnessed to a gigantic balloon that made him almost weightless.

Valencian priest Francisco Javier Serra (left) conducted an underwater reading of the Bible in September 2000. He and his two companions dived to a depth of 33 ft (10 m) in the Moraig creek off Alicante, Spain.

"Bible reading takes place 33 ft below water"

Some folks take car care a little too seriously! Torsten Baubach from Wales covered his mini with tiger print fur.

Don't Look Back Indian taxi driver Harpreet Devi is unique among cabbies—for he drives everywhere in reverse! He started driving backward when his car got stuck in reverse gear and he had to drive 35 mi (56 km) home. He has been driving his taxi in reverse for two years and has covered over 7,500 mi (12,070 km) at speeds of up to 25 mph (40 km/h).

Just Broken In In October 2003, 81-year-old Jusuf Sijaric from the town of Novi Pazar in southern Serbia revealed that he had been wearing the same pair of shoes for the past 60 years! He said he wanted to leave them to a museum when he dies.

Champion Liar In January 2003, Sandi Weld beat off several hundred rivals to become the winner of the 72nd World Champion Liar Contest by claiming that her sheep produced steel wool when she moved to Iron Mountain, Michigan.

Eight-year-olds Stephanie Larson (left) and Garrett Gilley won first place in the Tide Dirtiest Duo competition for children held in Santa Monica, California, in November 2000. Contestants had to tackle a stain-a-thon obstacle course ranging from chocolate pudding to peanut butter and jelly.

Dirty Diet Hao Fenglan, a 78-year-old Chinese woman has eaten dirt since the age of eight. In that time she has consumed over 10 tons of soil. She says she feels physical discomfort if she doesn't eat some dirt every day of her life.

Spirit of Give and Take North Carolina businessman Mike Jeffcoat played Santa over the Christmas holiday in 2002 by taping 300 $1 dollar bills to his office window accompanied by a note, which read: "Please take only what you need. Remember others." All the money had completely disappeared within 35 minutes.

Clowning Around In 2002, Spanish lawyer Alvaro Neil, 36, from Asturias, Spain, gave up his job and sold his car in order to cycle around South America dressed as a clown. Within 19 months he had ridden 19,200 mi (31,000 km) through ten countries.

Hidden Resident In July 2003, staff at a garbage dump in Berlin, Germany, discovered a man who had been living there undetected for ten years. His 3-ft (0.9-m) high hideaway contained a mattress, shelves, and a cupboard!

Feeling Peckish Gerben Hoeksma, 58, from the Netherlands, has a very unusual diet. For the past 11 years he has eaten three meals a day—of pigeon food. He says the meals are nutritious, healthy, appetizing, and cheap.

Lofty Intent In November 2002, pastor Steve Coad made his home on top of an advertising billboard above Highway 19 in Pinellas Park, Florida, and announced that he wouldn't be coming down until he had raised $23,000 for charity. He said: "I have a port-a-potty, a tent, a little TV, a mobile phone, baby wipes, toothpaste, and deodorant."

Singe Trim Bombay barber Aqueel Kiratpuri has abandoned using scissors to trim customers' hair in favor of burning the locks off with a candle flame. The "candle cut" revives an old Indian tradition and takes about an hour. It also reduces mess as the hair simply burns away.

Slice of Life Mike Uris from New Jersey ate a medium pizza and drank four diet cokes from the same take0ut stand almost every day for over five years. He estimated that between 1997 and 2002 he ate roughly 2,000 pizzas from his local Domino's store.

Out of Time Machine A Missouri man was found guilty of stealing transformers from a power company, with which he hoped to build a time machine that would help him predict future lottery numbers.

Brainstorm In October 2003, San Francisco artist Jonathan Keats registered his brain as a sculpture and began selling futures contracts on its six billion neurons, offering buyers the rights to any creativity it might produce if science learns how to keep it alive after his death.

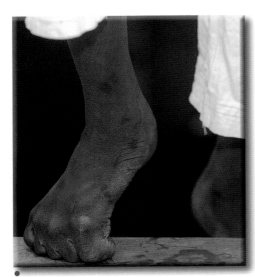

On March 27, 2003, K. Vasantha Kumar, a 25-year-old university student, walked up the 310 steps of a 16-story building in Madras, India, solely on his curled toes. The climb took him just three minutes.

DEVOTED TO DONUTS
Richard Ahern and his son Christopher spent two nights sleeping in a van in October 2002 just to make sure they would be the first people in Newington, Connecticut, to buy a new kind of donuts. The pair were first in the line when Krispy Kreme's new store opened, and were duly rewarded with a year's supply of donuts.

Echo Grey poses with her pet great dane, named Jagger, after the Fantasy Fest Pet Masquerade competition, which takes place annually at Key West, Florida. Grey airbrushed herself and Jagger so they looked like tigers and won a prize in the "most exotic" category.

Fruit takes on a new shape at a Tokyo market where cubic watermelons are sold.

Worrying Warrior

The Confederate army general Thomas "Stonewall" Jackson, who would not eat pepper because he thought it would hurt his left leg, always sat rigidly upright because he believed that his internal organs were misaligned, and rode into battle with his right arm held above his head, because he believed that it greatly improved the flow of blood to his brain.

Ultimate Squash In 2002, Jim Bristoe, a 42-year-old electrician from Elletsville, Indiana, built a cannon designed to fire a pumpkin one mile. With a 30-ft (9-m) barrel and powered by a 700-gal (2,600-l) air tank, the cannon is capable of blasting projectiles at a speed of 900 mph (1,450 km/h). During tests it fired a pumpkin through the rear of a Pontiac car!

Flying Finger Farhat Khan from India can type 60 words per minute using just one finger! He can also type in both Hindu and English at this speed.

" *Maize grew all over a man's body* "

Indian police constable Shyamial Bundele decided to lie down for days waiting for maize to grow over his mud-covered body! His objective for doing this was to raise money for the construction of a temple near Bhopal.

Churchgoers from a village in the Netherlands have created a replica of their local church—made from 10,000 Edam cheeses! The cheese church stands 13 ft (4 m) high and 30 ft (9 m) long!

Cow-Eyed A Missouri family woke one morning to find 13 eyeballs in their back yard! Tests revealed that they were from cows, but no one knew how they got there!

Time Traveler? Forty-four year old Andrew Carlssin made a $350 million fortune in just two weeks on Wall Street, having started with only $800! Not surprising, the Securities and Exchange Commission became suspicious and accused him of insider dealing. Carlssin made a four-hour long confession about how he was a time traveler from the year 2256 and so knew what the best investments were. Naturally the officials on the case weren't at all convinced of Carlssin's story, but it does seem strange that no record can be found of an Andrew Carlssin anywhere before he turned up as an adult in 2003!

Swallowing Pride For years, John "Red" Stuart of Philadelphia was the only man in the U.S. who could swallow an automobile axle. Now he has announced that because his Adam's apple has turned to bone, axles will no longer fit down his throat and he has decided it is safer to swallow samurai swords and bayonets!

Pet Pursuit To draw attention to his search for the family's missing pet dachshund, Summer Sausage, Rick Arbizzani of Florence, Illinois, took to the streets in 2003 dressed as Scooby Doo! Alas, nine months later there was still no sign of the dog.

Mayor Pays Up As the result of a lost bet in 2002, Mel Rothenburger, mayor of Kamloops in British Columbia, attended a council meeting dressed as a pink rabbit!

Ganesh Bhagat Chourasia, from Calcutta, suspends ten bricks weighing 77 lbs (35 kg) from his moustache. The shopkeeper is working toward lifting more than 110 lbs (50 kg)!

Raman Andiappan can husk a coconut with his teeth in 37.67 seconds. He is seen here demonstrating his skills in Madras, India!

Plane Crazy

Some couples choose to marry in the presence of Elvis, others choose to marry underwater, but these options were not exciting enough for Justin Bunn and Caroline Hackwood from Cirencester, England.

The bride and groom took their vows and were married by Reverend George Bingham while flying at 10,000 ft (3,050 m) over Rendcombe Airfield, England.

Justin Bunn and Caroline Hackwood got married while wing-walking on biplanes flying at great heights.

Something Borrowed

Japanese bride Yuko Osawa can afford to smile following her marriage to Ikuo Kine at Kakegawa City in 2000. For she was wearing the "Millennium Bra," spun in 24-carat gold thread, studded with 15 carats of diamonds and worth 200 million yen ($2 million).

This $2 million dollar bra, developed by lingerie maker Triumph® International Japan, was loaned to the Japanese couple for their wedding.

First Fight Newlyweds Marcia Alarcon and Carlos Alarcon-Schroder were jailed in Des Moines, Iowa, in 2001 after brawling over whose parents they would visit first!

Dig This Elaine Hesketh was expecting to leave the church at Manchester, England, in 2003, in a chauffeur-driven limousine—but instead traveled to the reception at 5 mph (8 km/h) while sitting in the bucket of a giant mechanical excavator. The unusual mode of transport was the idea of bridegroom Gary Hesketh, a former JCB driver (J.C. Bamford —makers of heavy-duty, drivable machinery).

Fit to be Tied Chinese bride Xu Fei is such a fitness fanatic that she wore a bikini on her wedding day in 2003 and performed an exercise workout for guests. She met her husband-to-be, Wang Xiaohu, at a gymnasium in Nanjing.

Set in Stone In 1976, Los Angeles secretary Jannene Swift officially married a 50-lb (23-kg) rock in a ceremony witnessed by over 20 people.

Bride Corinna Heimann and bridegroom Klaus Karrenberg prepare to climb down the 463-ft (141-m) high Frankfurt Office Center, Germany, during the 2001 skyscraper festival. A priest conducted their wedding ceremony at 98 ft (30 m) above the ground.

DROP-IN CEREMONY

Skydiving enthusiast Jason Stieneke found a novel way of arriving for his wedding to Peggy Sue Cordia in June 2002. He jumped from a plane and parachuted down to land on a lawn outside the church in Cape Girardeau, Missouri. Apart from a grass stain on his tuxedo, he was unhurt. The wedding photographer and best man also parachuted to the church, but the bride preferred to arrive by car.

One hundred and sixty couples from across China got married on October 12, 2002, in a mass wedding at the Juyongguan Pass on the Great Wall, north of Beijing. The event, the fourth of its kind on the Great Wall of China, was broadcast on the Internet.

Shotgun Wedding The Serbian wedding tradition of firing guns into the air in celebration brought an unexpected result in October 2003 when guests unwittingly shot down a small plane that had been flying low over the party at Ratina, near Belgrade.

Out of Place In 1993, a man shot a fellow guest dead at a wedding reception at Long Beach, California, because he was unhappy with the seating arrangements.

Nine-year-old Karnamoni Hasda (left) married a dog at a special ceremony at Khanyan, India, in June 2003. According to Santhal tribal custom, if a child's first tooth appears on the upper gum, he or she can only be saved from serious illness by marrying a dog.

Aged Divorce In 1984, 97-year-old Simon Stern from Wisconsin was divorced from his 91-year-old wife Ida.

Eli Cuellar (right) and her bridegroom Juan Videgain exchanged vows in an underwater aquarium of San Sebastian, northern Spain, on March 10, 2001.

" Underwater wedding ceremony "

In an Icy Grip

In 1914, relentless pack ice trapped the ship *Endurance* as Irish-born explorer Ernest Shackleton and his 27-man crew attempted to cross Antarctica. They spent the next four months marooned on an ice-floe.

Finally they took to lifeboats and made a perilous, nine-day voyage to Elephant Island. Shackleton then took five men in an open boat on a 17-day journey through some of the most stormy waters on Earth to South Georgia Island, where he led two of his men on a 36-hour trek over treacherous glaciers to reach a whaling station. He was able to borrow a ship in an attempt to rescue the remaining stranded crew members. He eventually reached the castaways on August 30, 1916. Amazingly, over the entire ordeal, not a single life was lost.

Shackleton borrowed a ship and spent the last four months of the ordeal trying to rescue the 22 men stranded on Elephant Island.

The Endurance *was trapped in pack ice and held for ten months before it finally sank.*

Meat on the Hoof During the French army's retreat from Moscow in the bitter winter of 1812, some soldiers survived by using their horses as living larders. They cut slices of flesh from their mounts to eat, but because the temperature was way below freezing, the blood froze instantly. The horses were so numb that they didn't feel pain.

Cold War Cow In November 1960, an American rocket launched from Cape Canaveral, Florida, veered off course and crashed in Cuba, killing a cow. The Cuban government gave the cow an official funeral as the victim of "imperialist aggression."

The Japanese television game show Endurance dared contestants who were brave enough to fight their fears, or carry out feats that pushed their strength and willpower to the very limits. Feats included hanging for hours on end with a cage of rats inches above, or being strapped into a box with live scorpions edging their way towards the contestants.

Baked Survivor In the summer of 1905, Mexican Pablo Valencia survived seven days in southwestern Arizona, without water, in temperatures up to 200°F (95°C). When he was found, his body was blackened and shrivelled, his eyes unblinking— but he recovered.

Tanya Streeter, seen here in a yoga pose, became the world's freediving champion in 2003. She was able to dive to depths of up to 525 ft (160 m) underwater.

Cut It Or Die
Rock climber Aran Ralston used a pen-knife to cut off part of his own arm to free himself after being trapped under a 1,000-lb (454-kg) boulder for five days in a canyon in Canyonlands National Park, Utah. Ralston was trapped on April 26, 2003, and spent three days trying to lever the boulder off himself. When his food ran out, he resorted to amputation. Carrying the severed limb, Ralston then careered 60 ft (18 m) to the bottom of the canyon and walked about 5 mi (8 km) before finding help.

Fifteen Weeks in Broken Boat

More than three months after setting out for a three-hour sail to Catalina Island in 2002, 62-year-old Richard van Pham of Long Beach, California, was rescued off the Pacific coast of Costa Rica. Van Pham had drifted more than 2,500 mi (4,000 km) south after a storm dismasted his boat, and his engine and radio failed. He survived on rainwater, fish, and turtles. When picked up by the United States patrol vessel *McClusky*, van Pham was grilling a seagull using wood from his own boat as fuel.

Van Pham (left) was rescued by the United States patrol vessel McClusky, *after being adrift for three and a half months.*

Richard van Pham spent his time adrift off the Pacific coast in this battered sailboat, which had been damaged by high winds.

Up and Away In 1979, Peter Strelzyk and Guenter Wetzel and their families escaped from Communist East Berlin in a hot-air balloon stitched together from curtains and bedsheets, and inflated with a home-made gas burner.

Ski Plunge In extreme skiing, which involves hurtling down near-vertical slopes, Harry Egger of Austria set a world record, reaching speeds of 155 mph (250 km/h) in 1999.

Faithful Mailman August Sutter, aged 83, delivered mail over the same route in rural Illinois for 64 years, covering more than a million miles in this time!

During an aborted 1975 space mission, the Russian crew of Soyuz-18A endured forces of 21 G—five times greater than the G-forces that cosmonauts must withstand during routine maneuvers.

Air Drop American round-the-world balloonist Steve Fossett was rescued uninjured from the Coral Sea after his hot-air balloon ruptured at an altitude of 29,000 ft (8,840 m).

Aargh A 62-year-old Korean man choked to death after swallowing a live octopus—which is a popular snack in Korea. The octopus was still alive when doctors removed it.

Hold Your Breath The Ama pearl divers of Japan make up to 100 dives each day to depths of around 66 ft (20 m) without suffering ill-effects.

Mid-Air Grab Thrown out of his exploding bomber in April 1944, Australian pilot Joe Herman struck something in mid-air. Grabbing the object he had collided with, Herman found himself hanging onto the legs of upper gunner John Vivash, whose parachute had just opened. Both men landed under the single parachute, sustaining only minor injuries.

SOFT LANDING

RAF Flight Sergeant Nicholas Alkemade was on a bombing mission over Germany in 1944 when his Lancaster bomber was hit by enemy fire. Faced with the choice of burning to death in the blazing bomber or jumping without a parachute from 18,000 ft (5,486 m), Alkemade chose to jump. He passed out during the fall and woke to find himself in a snowdrift, with only a twisted ankle, tree branches having broken his fall. The hardest part was convincing the German patrol that found him how he came to be there without a parachute.

Tragic Ascent In 1875, French scientist Gaston Tissandier made a balloon ascent to about 35,000 ft (10,700 m). Although the balloon was equipped with primitive oxygen equipment, Tissandier and his two colleagues lost consciousness before they could use it. Tissandier survived, but both his companions perished.

Man Whips Horse In 2002, American sprinter Tom Johnson raced a horse and rider for 50 mi (31 km) across a desert in the United Arab Emirates. Johnson came home in 5 hours, 45 minutes, beating the horse by just 10 seconds. The horse had stopped for an hour during the race to eat, drink, and rest.

Jet Chokes On June 24, 1982, a British Airways Boeing 747 cruising at an altitude of 37,000 ft (11,278 m) flew through a volcanic ash plume from Galanggung volcano on Java. Ash sucked into the engines caused all four engines to cut out. The plane went into a steep glide for 15 minutes, dropping to 13,000 ft (3,962 m), but at the last minute Captain Eric Moody and his crew were able to restart the engines and make an emergency landing at Jakarta airport.

Epic Journey Home In February 1924, six months after Frank and Elizabeth Brazier lost their pet collie Bobbie in Wolcott, Indiana, the dog turned up back home in Silverton, Oregon, having made an incredible 3,000 mi (4,830 km) journey.

The Ultimate Leap On August 16, 1960, Colonel Joseph W. Kittinger Jr. jumped from a balloon at 102,800 ft (31,333 m)—more than 19 mi (31 km) high—to set the high altitude parachute jump world record. It took Colonel Kittinger more than 13 minutes to finally reach the ground.

Hans Graas saved his three companions when they plunged into a crevice from a rock projection while climbing the 12,834-ft (3,912-m) Piz Palu mountain in Switzerland. Graas saved them by leaping off the other side of the rock as they fell, in order to create a balance by counter-pulling on the rope to which they were all attached, preventing them from all falling off the one side.

While journeying around the world, British yachtsman Tony Bullimore (right) survived for five days trapped under his boat after it capsized in the icy Southern Ocean in 1997.

Women Conquer Asia

It took four British women, Sophia Cunningham, Lucy Kelaart, Alexandra Tolstoy, and Victoria Westmacott, eight months to ride horses and camels across Uzbekistan, Kygyzstan, and two-thirds of China, traveling over four deserts and two mountain ranges on horse- and camel-back.

While on their 4,300-mi (6,920-km) journey, the women experienced extremes of temperature, frozen contact lenses, and Chinese shepherds eager to trade 1,000 camels for one of the girls!

The four intrepid travelers arrived in Xi'an, China, on their camels after the adventurous eight-month journey.

High-flying Hobo A 23-year-old Chinese man, on July 29, 1998, survived temperatures of about –80°F (–50°C) and a shortage of oxygen at an altitude of 32,800 ft (9,998 m) in the wheel well of a jumbo jet. The man was on a three-hour flight from Shanghai to Tokyo.

CRAWL FOR LIFE

While descending from the summit of Siula Grande, a 20,850-ft (6,355-m) peak in the Peruvian Andes, British climber Joe Simpson fell and smashed his knee. His partner, Simon Yates, lowered Simpson down the mountain on a rope, but Simpson slipped over the edge of a cliff and plunged into a deep crevasse. Yates had little choice but to cut the rope to avoid being pulled down himself. After a long, fruitless search for Simpson's body Yates returned to base camp, about 6 mi (10 km) away. Miraculously, Simpson had survived the fall, and in the next three days he pulled himself out of the crevasse and crawled back to base camp.

Thin Air Pioneers In 1862 British balloonists James Glaischer and Henry Coxwell ascended to a height of 28,770 ft (8,770 m) without oxygen—nearly the same altitude as the summit of Mount Everest.

This Mahatma Gandhi devotee painted himself silver to symbolize a statue, and walked for nearly 100 mi (160 km) in India in 1992 to commemorate Gandhi's famous Freedom March.

Ignoring the Cold
A Nepalese pilgrim who followed a 1960 American expedition in the Himalayas walked barefoot in the snow at 15,000 ft (4,570 m). He slept in the open in temperatures that fell to −20°F (−30°C), wearing only cotton pants, a shirt, and an overcoat.

Interrupted Nap
Chad Dillon from Indiana was in a dumpster, sleeping off a big night out, when he was collected by a garbage truck. He managed to escape when his screams were heard. He had head, chest, and arm injuries from being compacted three times.

Taking the Heat
In an 18th-century experiment, an English scientist named Blagden voluntarily shut himself in a room that had been heated to 221°F (105°C)! With him he had a dog, some eggs, and a piece of raw steak. Fifteen minutes later, Blagden and the dog emerged unharmed, but the eggs had been baked hard and the steak cooked.

LAST MAN STANDING
Japanese soldier Lt. Hiroo Onoda refused to surrender for 29 years after World War II was over, claiming that stories of Japan's defeat were propaganda. It wasn't until his former commanding officer flew to Lubang, the remote Philippines island where Onoda was holed up, and ordered him to lay down his arms, that he finally emerged from the jungle on March 19, 1972.

Bungee Ticket
A Canadian man was arrested after trying, without success, to bungee jump onto a cruise ship passing under a Vancouver bridge.

Thawed Out Well
Anna Bagenholm, a 29-year-old Norwegian skier, was trapped in an icy river for more than an hour. By the time she was rescued, her body temperature had fallen to 57°F (14°C)—that's 43°F (23°C) below normal. Pronounced clinically dead, she was taken to Tromso University Hospital where a resuscitation team managed to revive her. Eight months later, the only lingering effect was a tingling in Anna's fingers.

Double Miracle
Juliane Koepcke, a German teenager, had not one but two miraculous escapes after the airliner she was on broke up in a storm over Peru on Christmas Eve, 1971. First, she survived the fall of more than 10,000 ft (3,000 m). Then, despite a broken collarbone and other injuries, she walked for 11 days through the rainforest before finally finding help.

Seventy-six year old Indian, Prahlad Jani, claims to have survived 68 years without eating or drinking. A band of devotees have formed to pay homage to this man who claims his survival under such circumstances is due to divine inspiration. To prove his claim of surviving without food or drink, he agreed to go under surveillance at his local hospital, where they were unable to refute his claims.

Fire in the Hole In 1993, Stanley Williams, an American volcanologist, was taking measurements inside the Colombian volcano Galeras when it erupted, incinerating six of his colleagues and three tourists. Fiery debris fractured Williams' skull and broke his legs, but two female fellow volcanologists braved the explosion and mounted an amazing rescue effort to carry him off the mountain.

Speed Climb Most climbers take four days to reach the summit of Mt. Everest from Base Camp, but in May 2003, Sherpa Lhakpa Gelu made the ascent in just under 11 hours, beating the previous best time—also held by a Sherpa—by nearly two hours.

Indonesian magician Alford escaped from chains and shackles while immersed in a tank full of sharks at Seaworld in Jakarta in June 2003. He was underwater for a total of 1 min, 50 sec.

❝ *Walked a tightrope for 22 days* ❞

Chinese tightrope walker Adili Wushouer in 2002 stayed on a tightrope above Jinghai Lake in the suburbs of Beijing, for 22 days.

Russian Michail Lasjuv learned to read braille using his lips after losing his hands, vision, and hearing during World War II.

Girl Tackles Python Six-year-old Marlie Coleman of Cairns, Australia, was awarded the RSPCA's humane award for saving her kitten from a scrub python in 2003. The python had grabbed her kitten Sooty in her backyard, and when Marlie tried to make it let go, it sank its teeth into her lip, hanging on until Marlie's mother heard the screams and shook the snake off.

Steady Climb Matthew Palframan, a dyslexic who could not speak until he was three years old and who, as an adult, only has the reading age of a child, won a place at Oxford University, England, in 2002 to study chemistry.

Genius Dreamer Albert Einstein, one of the greatest scientists of all time, was described by a teacher as "mentally slow, unsociable, and adrift forever in his foolish dreams."

Julius Rosenburg, age 5, of Winnipeg, Manitoba, Canada, snatched his three-year-old sister from the jaws of a bear then growled at the animal until it fled.

Slow Start As a student John Maynard Keynes, one of the most influential economists of the 20th century, regularly got the lowest marks in his economics class.

Jim Abbott, born with only one hand, became a major league baseball player in the 1990s. Among the teams he pitched for were the California Angels, the New York Yankees, and the Chicago White Sox. During his career he pitched a no-hitter.

Diving Champ At the age of 90, Viola Krahn won the 10 ft (3-m) springboard diving competition at the United States Master's Indoor Championships in Brown Deer, Wisconsin.

Mini-Grandmaster In 2002, Sergei Karjakin, a 12-year-old Ukrainian boy, became the youngest grandmaster in chess history.

Early Starter Wolfgang Amadeus Mozart composed his first piano pieces at the age of five years!

Red Bottom Line

A Bolivian street vendor hangs out red underwear in preparation for the New Year season's increase in sales.

In some countries, such as Bolivia, many people wear red underwear on New Year's Eve, as it is believed to bring good luck in the following year.

In Poland, red underwear has also been accredited with helping to bring success to students writing exams. A study published in the Polish media in 2003 reported that students wearing red underwear were more likely to pass their exams than fellow students sticking to more conservative colors. Lingerie shops in Poland saw a huge increase of sales as students flocked to buy red underwear in a bid to guarantee exam success!

Lucky the chicken survived a truck crash in 2002 that killed 2,000 chickens on board. He fled into the undergrowth when the truck overturned on the highway on its way to the slaughterhouse.

Dave Clements was extremely lucky when he survived a fall in 2001 after his parachute failed to open. His fall was broken when he landed on an aircraft hangar, leaving him with just a fractured arm.

Lottery Lifesaver Patrick Gayle of Harrisburg, Pennsylvania, survived being shot at when a bullet lodged in 80 lottery tickets that were stuffed in his breast pocket.

Good Luck Fails An Italian man picked a four-leaf clover on a clifftop in Vibo Marina, then slipped on the wet grass and plunged 150 ft (46 m) to his death.

Price of Greed In 1977, a man was knocked down by a car in New York, but fortunately was uninjured. A bystander told him it would be a good idea to pretend he was hurt and claim the insurance money, so he lay down in front of the car again. No sooner had he done so than the car rolled forward and crushed him to death.

Safe and Warm Twenty-seven percent of past female winners of the British National Lottery keep their winning tickets in their bras.

Poor Judgment A 25-year-old motorist in New Zealand was driving to court to face a charge of driving while under suspension, when he crashed into a car driven by a man who turned out to be the judge assigned to hear his case.

Ill-Fated Revival When a New York woman was pronounced dead from heart disease, preparations for her burial began. At the funeral parlor she "came back to life," sat up in her coffin, and asked what was going on. The woman's daughter promptly dropped dead of shock.

Choice Number The number seven is the most popular number chosen by lottery players.

Bruiser the dog fell 200 ft (61 m) from a cliff in Dorset, England, but miraculously survived!

Bite Worse than Bark A beech tree near a churchyard in Suffolk, England, had a skull carved in its trunk, and many villagers thought it was cursed. A local farmer cut down the tree, sceptical of the curse. He cut his hand badly on his chainsaw, and when he stepped on a nail, his foot turned septic. He developed jaundice and was rushed to the hospital, where he died.

Shortlived Triumph In Foggia, Italy, Armando Pinelli, 70, won his argument with another man over who should sit in the only chair in the shade of a palm tree, but when he sat down, the tree toppled over and killed him.

Single Strokes of Luck

The odds of hitting a hole-in-one in golf are 1 in 15,000—but some lucky golfers manage to achieve this, including five-year-old Mason Aldrege who, in 2002, hit a 106-yd (97-m) hole-in-one at Eagle's Bluff Country Club in Bullard, Texas. However, the record for the youngest golfer to hit a hole-in-one is held by three-year-old Jake Paine of Orange County, California. A much older, 76-year-old Felicity Sieghart hit two holes-in-one in the same round at Aldeburgh Golf Club, England, in 2003.

In 2001, lucky eight-year-old Greg Law scored a hole-in-one at Oldmeldrum Club in Scotland.

Lip Reading Micaela Velasco, 101 years old, was declared dead by a doctor in Zamora, north-west Spain. A few hours later, undertakers were preparing her for burial when they saw her lips move. Three days later, she was "as fit as a lady of her age can be."

Gee, Thanks After purchasing countless losing raffle tickets, balding Chris Calver of Newcastle–upon–Tyne, England, finally struck lucky, winning some curling tongs.

Next Stop Jail A man in Rio de Janeiro who robbed bus passengers of more than $800 (£470) alighted at the next stop only to be arrested by the commanding officer of more than 400 police officers gathered for a ceremony.

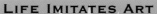

Mohammad Nasib from Pakistan tells the fortune of customers who pass by in the street, using his talking fortune-telling parrots!

LIFE IMITATES ART

In Edgar Allan Poe's 1838 fictional story *The Narrative of Arthur Gordon Pym of Nantucket,* four men adrift in a boat kill and eat a cabin boy called Richard Parker. Forty-six years later, the real-life crew of the *Mignonette* were cast adrift after their ship was sunk in a storm. After 19 days without food, the captain decided to kill and eat the 17-year-old cabin boy, whose body kept the sailors alive for 35 days until they were rescued. The unfortunate boy's name was Richard Parker.

Lovelorn Leap Devastated by her husband's suspected adultery, Vera Czermak of Prague, Czech Republic, jumped from her third-story window—and accidentally landed on him as he passed below. She recovered in hospital, but he died instantly.

Body Armor Jane Selma Soares, a Brazilian woman shot in crossfire between police and drug dealers in 2002, was saved by her silicone breast implants, which slowed the bullet up enough to prevent it from causing her serious injury.

Bank-Breaking Labor In 1873, Englishman Joseph Jaggers "broke the bank" at the Beaux-Arts Casino, Monte Carlo. It wasn't just luck. Jaggers spent time figuring out that one of the six roulette wheels was unbalanced, throwing up nine numbers more often than natural probability indicated. By the time the casino figured out Jaggers' system and redesigned the wheel, he had netted the astonishing amount of $325,000!

Hail Attack Almost 5,000 holes the size of baseballs were made in a biplane during a freak hailstorm. The pilot managed somehow to fly his plane 275 mi (445 km) to land safely.

Superstitious President Franklin D. Roosevelt was a sufferer of triskaidekaphobia— the fear of the number thirteen. Incidentally, eleven plus two is an anagram of twelve plus one.

Sticky Situation Bill the plumber had to be freed by firemen after he got his head stuck in a lavatory bowl at his house in Puckeridge, Hertfordshire, England. His full name was W.C. Sticks.

War Victim The first bomb dropped by the Allies on Berlin during World War II killed the only elephant in the city's Zoo.

Sight Shock Nine years after being blinded in an accident, Edwin Robinson of Falmouth, Maine, recovered his sight after being struck by lightning on June 4, 1980.

Streaks of Luck

Bill Morgan's extraordinary run of good luck began in 1998, when the Australian truck driver won a car in a scratch lottery. He was asked to re-enact his scratchcard triumph for the benefit of a local TV station, and won another AU$250,000 (US$173,000 / £121,000) on the scratch card there and then! A spokesman for the lottery said the odds of winning both prizes were more than six billion to one. Croatian Frane Selak, over the course of ten years, escaped relatively unharmed from a train accident, a bus accident, falling from a plane, three car fires, and being knocked down by a bus in Zagreb, Croatia. Selak's extraordinary run of luck reached its peak when, in 2003, he won the Croatian lottery, winning the equivalent of $1 million!

" Kitten survives 105°F wash cycle! "

RETURN OF THE RING

A gold ring lost at a swimming pool in Colchester, England, turned up 27 years later inside an apple. The ring was discovered in 2002 by 12-year-old Jamie-Louisa Arnold when she bit into the apple. Rosalind Pike saw the ring in a press photograph and immediately recognized it as the one that she had lost during a school swimming trip in 1975. A gardening expert suggested that a bird might have picked up the ring and dropped it in an orchard, and the apple formed around it.

Sugar, an extremely lucky 12-month-old kitten, survived inside a washing machine for 45 minutes at 105°F (40°C) after accidentally being shut in the machine.

Index

Index

ACKNOWLEDGMENTS

Jacket (b/l) Philip Dunn/Rex Features

7 (t/r) PNS/REX, (b) Roman Soumar/CORBIS; 8 (t) Peter Turnley/CORBIS; 9 (t) AFP/GETTYIMAGE; 10 (b) IPC Magazines:Whats On TV/REX; 11 (t) Bettmann/CORBIS; 13 (b) AFP/GETTYIMAGE; 14 (b) J.G. Morell/AFP/GETTYIMAGE; 15 (t) SWS/REX, (b) John T.Barr/AFP/GETTYIMAGE; 16 (l/c) Dibyangshu Sarkar/AFP/ GETTYIMAGE, (b/r) Andy Newman/AFP/GETTYIMAGE; 17 (t) Jiji Press/AFP/GETTYIMAGE, (b) AFP/GETTYIMAGE; 18 (t/l) Jeroen Oerlemans/REX; (b/l) Dibyangshu Sarkar/AFP/GETTYIMAGE; (b/r) Sourvav/AFP/GETTYIMAGE; 19 (c) Peter Macdiarmid/REX; 20 (t) Yoshikazu Tsuno/AFP/GETTYIMAGE, (b) Katja Lenz-Pool/AFP/GETTYIMAGE; 21 (t) AFP/GETTYIMAGE, (l/c) Deshakal Yan Chowdhury/AFP/GETTYIMAGE, (b) AFP/GETTYIMAGE; 22 (t/r) Pictorial Press Ltd, (b) Pictorial Press Ltd; 23 (t) Philip Dunn/REX, (b) Christophe Simon/AFP/GETTYIMAGE; 24 (t) AFP/GETTYIMAGE, (c/r) AFP/GETTYIMAGE, (b) NASA/AFP/GETTYIMAGE; 25 (r) AFP/GETTYIMAGE, (b) AFP/GETTYIMAGE; 26 (b) Lucy Kelaart/REX; 27 (t) Lindsey Hebberd/CORBIS, (b) AFP/GETTYIMAGE; 28 (t) Bay Ismoyo/AFP/GETTYIMAGE, (b) AFP/GETTYIMAGE; 29 (b) John Zich/AFP/GETTYIMAGE; 30 (t) AFP/GETTYIMAGE, (b) Paul Watts/REX; 31 (t) Jeremy Durkin/REX, (b) Matt Morton/REX; 32 (t) Helen Osler/REX, (b) Jewel Samad/AFP/GETTYIMAGE;   33 (b) Neil Hall/REX

All other photos are from Corel, PhotoDisc, Digtial Vision and Ripley's Entertainment Inc.